VOLCANOES

MICHAEL WOODS AND MARY B WOODS

LERNER BOOKS • LONDON • NEW YORK • MINNEAPOLIS

To Caden Samuel Woods

Editor's note: Determining the exact death toll following disasters is often difficult – if not impossible – especially in the case of disasters that took place long ago. The authors and the editors in this series have used their best judgement in determining which figures to include.

First published in the United Kingdom in 2008 by
Lerner Books,
Dalton House,
60 Windsor Avenue,
London SW19 2RR

Website address: www.lernerbooks.co.uk

This edition was updated and edited for UK publication by Discovery Books Ltd.,
Unit 3, 37 Watling Street, Leintwardine, Shropshire SY7 0LW

British Library Cataloguing in Publication Data

Woods, Michael
  Volcanoes. - (Disasters up close)
  1. Volcanic eruptions - Juvenile literature 2.
Volcanoes -
  Juvenile literature
  I. Title II. Woods, Mary B.
  363.3'495

ISBN-13: 978 1 58013 458 3

Printed in China

Contents

Introduction

THURSDAY 17 JANUARY 2002, WAS A NORMAL DAY IN GOMA. THIS CITY OF ABOUT 400,000 PEOPLE IS IN AFRICA'S DEMOCRATIC REPUBLIC OF CONGO (FORMERLY ZAIRE). CHILDREN WERE AT SCHOOL, ADULTS WERE GOING ABOUT THEIR BUSINESS AND EVERYONE WAS LOOKING FORWARD TO A PLEASANT WEEKEND.

Residents of Goma trudged across piles of cooling lava after the 2002 eruption of Mount Nyiragongo.

Suddenly nearby Mount Nyiragongo turned the normal day into a nightmare. Nyiragongo is a 'fire mountain' – a volcano. At 9.30 am, it erupted, belching out gas, dust and huge rivers of red-hot lava (melted rock). These fiery rivers flowed towards Goma – just 18 kilometres (11 miles) away.

'THE THING THAT ATE GOMA'

'From the air it looked like an octopus with massive spreading tentacles uncoiled across miles of verdant, green jungle,' said Wendy Driscoll. Wendy worked for CARE International, an agency that helps disaster victims.

Everything the foul-smelling lava touched – grass, houses, animals and people – burned. Some lava rivers flowed at 100 kmph, as fast as cars on a main road. The lava was too fast for some people to get away. They were trapped and burned to death.

'The destruction here is on a scale which is overwhelming,' said Sally Sara, a reporter. 'Lava has gushed through the streets, seeping into the buildings and taking with it anything it could carry. Cars, trucks . . . and bricks are now embedded in the hot rock.'

After the eruption, the lava was 2 metres thick in some parts of Goma. It cooled into rock as crisp as egg shells. 'Each footstep sounds like walking on glass or gravel,' Sara said. 'Locals move quickly. . . . People walk in fast motion, like characters from an old silent movie.'

The Mount Nyiragongo eruption killed about 45 people and injured hundreds more. Many had terrible burns that left scars on their faces and bodies. The disaster also destroyed most of Goma and fourteen nearby villages. More than 200,000 people lost their homes.

Fire mountains are dangerous and fascinating. Volcanic eruptions occur all over the world. They will cause disasters in the future. These disasters will affect the lives of real people, just like the people of Goma.

'If this were a movie,
it would be called
"The Thing That Ate Goma."'

– Wendy Driscoll, an aid worker, describing the lava that streamed towards Goma (above)

What Are Volcanoes?

A VOLCANO IS AN OPENING IN THE EARTH'S SURFACE THAT RELEASES RED-HOT MELTED ROCK, GASES, ASH AND CHUNKS OF ROCK. THE OPENING FORMS WHEN MELTED ROCK, OR MAGMA, MOVES UP THROUGH THE EARTH FROM FAR BELOW THE SURFACE.

Some volcanoes are vents – holes or cracks in the ground, but many are cone-shaped mountains. In fact, some of the most beautiful mountains in the world are volcanoes. They include Mount Fuji in Japan and Mount Saint Helens in the US state of Washington.

FIERY FOUNTAINS AND STINKING GASES

Volcanic eruptions are among the most violent events on Earth. They sometimes include tremendous explosions. As magma rises underground, the earth often trembles and shakes.

During an eruption, fountains of lava shoot out of the volcano and fly through the air. Lava also flows along the ground – sometimes very slowly, but at other times as fast as 55 to 100 kmph. Hot volcanic gases include sulphur, which stinks of rotten eggs.

GOOD-BYE, T REX

Talk about disasters! Some scientists think that huge volcanic eruptions killed 70 per cent of all plants and animals on Earth – including the dinosaurs – about 65 million years ago. Dust from the eruptions may have blocked out sunlight and killed the plants that animals needed for food. The dust might have made the Earth too cold for dinosaurs (*left*) and other animals to survive.

Mount Fuji makes a dramatic backdrop to the Japanese landscape. Fuji last erupted in 1707.

Blasts of these gases send rocks the size of bowling balls flying into the air. Burning-hot volcanic ash falls like snow. Ash can pile up so deeply that it collapses roofs on houses, buries buildings and blocks roads.

GREATEST DISASTERS

Volcanic eruptions have caused some of the world's worst disasters. These events have caused great destruction. A volcanic eruption in a wild area where nobody lives is an environmental disaster, damaging land and trees. When a volcanic eruption causes harm to people, buildings, roads or bridges, it becomes a human disaster.

About ten major volcanic eruptions occur each year. People living near volcanoes can be killed or injured, or they may lose their homes. In the last three hundred years alone, volcanoes have killed more than 260,000 people. Volcanoes have been a danger to humans for much longer than that. Over thousands of years, they have destroyed cities and changed landscapes.

A Japanese man walked through a doorway in his house, which was half-filled with volcanic ash from Mount Unzen in 1993.

THE YEAR WITHOUT A SUMMER

The eruption of Indonesia's Mount Tambora in the spring of 1815 was one of the biggest volcanic eruptions in the last ten thousand years. Dust from Mount Tambora temporarily blocked out sunlight, making global weather unusually cold for more than a year. Cold temperatures and heavy rainfall resulted in poor harvests in Britain. Frost killed farmers' crops in Indonesia and beyond. People went hungry and some starved to death. At least 92,000 people died.

A vehicle escaping from a billowing cloud of ash during the 1991 eruption of Mount Pinatubo, a volcano in the Philippines.

' *A furious volcano.*
A trembling earth.
A black hole. '

— reporter Susan Kreifels, describing Mount Pinatubo

The effects of an eruption can also be felt far from the volcano. Dust and ash from a large eruption may encircle the globe. This material can stay in the atmosphere for years and even change the Earth's climate. For example, in the summer of 1991, Mount Pinatubo (in the Philippines) and Mount Hudson (in Chile, South America) both erupted. Together, these two volcanoes poured enough dust into the air to block out sunlight and temporarily cool global temperatures.

Although volcanic eruptions can be very destructive, they sometimes have good effects. Volcanic ash makes soil more fertile for farming, and when lava flows into the oceans, it can form new land. Eruptions of Hawaii's Mount Kilauea have formed new coastal land roughly as big as six hundred football pitches! Undersea volcanic eruptions build new islands in the same way – from the bottom up. The Hawaiian Islands were formed millions of years ago by eruptions of submarine (underwater) volcanoes.

INVISIBLE DANGERS

Volcanoes release gases that are invisible but very dangerous. They can poison and kill nearby plants, animals and people. They also add to air pollution. The gases mix with volcanic ash, making the dark 'smoke' that billows from some erupting volcanoes.

Hot lava steams as it pours into the coastal waters of Hawaii.

Crops thrive in the rich volcanic soil near the Merapi volcano, on the Indonesian island of Java.

Mount Vesuvius and
Pompeii's ruins

AD 79
MOUNT VESUVIUS

The 24 August, AD 79, was an ordinary day in the ancient Roman towns of Pompeii and Herculaneum. The people of these towns, which were part of the ancient Roman Empire in what became modern Italy, went about their day-to-day lives. Nearby Mount Vesuvius had been rumbling lately, but that wasn't unusual. No one was worried.

Suddenly, Vesuvius exploded. It buried Pompeii and Herculaneum under boiling hot mud and ash. One eyewitness was a young student named Gaius Plinius Caecilius Secundus (Pliny the Younger).

He was staying with his mother and uncle, Pliny the Elder, about 30 km (18 miles) away from the mountain. *'On Mount Vesuvius broad sheets of fire and leaping flames blazed,' Gaius wrote. 'On the landward side a fearful black cloud was rent by forked and quivering bursts of flame, and parted to reveal great tongues of fire, like flashes of lightning magnified in size.'*

Then the cloud began moving towards Gaius. His mother was too old to run quickly and begged her son to leave her behind. *'I refused to save myself without her, and grasping her hand forced her to quicken her pace, a dense black cloud was coming up behind us, spreading over the earth like a flood.'*

Gaius and his mother escaped. His uncle and hundreds of other people were not so lucky. They were trapped as hot ash and rocks poured down from the sky. *'As a protection against falling objects they put pillows on their heads,'* Gaius said. But for those closest to the mountain, such protection was not enough. More than 3,000 people died.

This eruption has taught us a lot about life in the Roman Empire. Mud and ash buried people in Pompeii and Herculaneum in the middle of their everyday lives, freezing everything in time. The eruption gave us a snapshot of daily life more than two thousand years ago,

This ancient portrait shows Terentius Neo and his wife, who lived in Pompeii before the eruption.

'**You could hear the shrieks of women, the wailing of infants, and the shouting of men....**'

– Pliny the Younger

with information about what people ate, how they dressed and how they decorated their homes.

Mount Vesuvius remains one of the Earth's most dangerous volcanoes. Some scientists say it is the most dangerous of all. It has erupted more than fifty times since AD 79, and more than 2 million people live within its range. Any future eruption would be a very great disaster.

The bodies of Vesuvius's victims decayed over the years, leaving spaces in the hardened mud. This lifelike cast was made from filling one of those spaces with plaster.

How Volcanoes Form

THE EARTH'S CORE IS HOT ENOUGH TO MELT ROCK INTO A THICK RED LIQUID CALLED MAGMA. VOLCANOES FORM WHEN MAGMA RISES TO THE EARTH'S SURFACE THROUGH VENTS.

Magma rises because it is lighter than the surrounding rock. The magma's heat melts more of the rock around it, creating hollow underground chambers (spaces). As more and more magma pours into a chamber, the pressure inside builds up – almost like the pressure from blowing up a balloon. If the pressure gets high enough, magma will burst up and out through the Earth's surface. This bursting forth of melted rock, hot gases, ash and chunks of dirt and stone is an eruption.

Once magma reaches the Earth's surface, it is called lava. The lava gradually cools, changing back into solid rock. As this rock piles up around a vent, it can form a cone-shaped mountain. Falling ash also adds to a volcano's growth.

Some volcanoes, including Mount Kilauea in Hawaii, ooze lava quietly for long periods of time. Others, such as Mount Saint Helens, in the United States, occasionally erupt with violent explosions.

IT'S A GAS!

Did you know that magma is like a fizzy drink? Both contain dissolved gases. The fizz in drinks comes from carbon dioxide. Magma contains poisonous gases. Underground, pressure keeps the gas inside the magma. At the Earth's surface, that pressure is released. Gases bubble out, splattering lava *(above)* like a fizzy drink from a shaken can.

CROSS SECTION OF A VOLCANO

gas, ash and rock

crater

magma

lava

magma chamber

VOLCANOES ON A PLATE

The Earth's shell, or crust, is not solid all the way through. Beneath the surface we walk on, the crust is made up of gigantic floating chunks of rock called tectonic plates. Most volcanoes are located near the edges of these plates.

The Earth's surface has seven main plates and many smaller ones. Each plate is about 80 km (50 miles) thick. The plates float on magma, almost like leaves floating on a puddle of water. All the Earth's continents sit on top of these plates.

Tectonic plates are always moving. In some places, they slowly shift away from one another. In other spots, plates move towards one another, or one plate might sink down below another. Volcanoes tend to occur at the borders between plates. Other volcanoes, however, are far away from the edges of tectonic plates. They form where unusually hot magma melts right through the Earth's surface. Experts call these places hot spot volcanoes.

LAVA, ASH AND MUD

Many people think that flowing lava is the most dangerous part of a volcanic eruption. It can be as hot as 1100°C, burning everything it touches. When a lava flow goes through a town, it can start fires and cause great destruction. Lava, however, is actually not the biggest volcano hazard.

FIRE GODS

The word *volcano* comes from Vulcan, the Roman god of fire. The ancient Romans believed this god lived under Vulcano, an island off the coast of Italy *(above, right)*. The island's volcano was said to be the chimney Vulcan used as he made thunderbolts and swords.

The ancient Greek god of fire was Hephaestus. The Greeks believed he served as the jail keeper of a giant named Typhon. Zeus, king of the gods, had imprisoned Typhon under Mount Etna in Italy. Etna rumbled when Hephaestus hammered iron swords and spears. Eruptions occurred whenever Typhon tried to escape.

16

A column of ash rises into the
sky from a volcano in the Azores,
a group of Atlantic islands that
are part of Portugal.

Imagine a huge grey cloud of hot ash, rock and gas rushing outwards from a volcano and billowing down the street. It is hot enough to make paper burst into flame, and it moves as fast as 160 kmph. This cloud is called a pyroclastic flow. Pyroclastic flows move like liquid. They may travel further than 50 km (30 miles) from a volcano. Anything and everything in a flow's path is in danger – buildings, cars, trees, crops, animals and people.

Now try to imagine a wall of mud coming right towards your house. Along its path, it may pick up sharp stones and broken tree branches that scratch and cut. This scary sight is a lahar. Lahars – also called mudflows – are like pyroclastic flows, but they contain water. A lahar may form when a pyroclastic flow collects water by crossing a river or lake. Mudflows can also occur when an eruption's heat melts snow and ice on a volcano's peak. In 1985 lahars caused by the eruption of the Nevado del Ruiz volcano (in Colombia, South America) killed more than 20,000 people. Hundreds of houses were buried – with many of their owners still inside.

CURSE OF THE VOLCANO GODDESS

'Okay to take this home?' asked a visitor to the Hawaiian Volcano Observatory (HVO) near Mount Kilauea. He held up a beautiful piece of hardened lava. 'Take it if you dare,' replied Doctor Robert Tilling, an HVO scientist. 'But Pele may get angry.' Doctor Tilling explained the ancient legend of Pele. According to Hawaiian legends, Pele is a moody and powerful volcano goddess who causes eruptions. Volcanic rocks *(below)* are her prized possessions, and she gets angry with people who take them. Some people who have taken rocks home have had bad luck. Blaming Pele, many of these people mailed the rocks back to Hawaii – sometimes with a note apologizing to the volcano goddess.

Lahars *(below)* from Nevado del Ruiz devastated the town of Armero, Colombia, in 1985. The mudflows buried homes, schools and shops, leaving thousands dead and many more homeless.

' *The mud grabbed me and pushed me under.*
I would come up again and again.
It dragged me about two miles.
The mud was in my nose, mouth and ears.
I couldn't breathe. '

– Modesto Menesses,
an Armero taxi driver who survived the Nevado del Ruiz eruption

TERRIBLE TEPHRA

A material called tephra, which is hurled into the air during an eruption, is also dangerous. Tephra contains dust-like specks of ash. It also includes huge rocks the size of footballs, which can smash things 65 km (40 miles) away.

Although each piece of ash is very small, ash can cause great damage. It sometimes picks up an electric charge in the atmosphere around a volcano, triggering deadly lightning bolts.

Aeroplane pilots dread volcanic ash. Clouds of ash in the air can clog aeroplane engines. After the 1982 eruption of Indonesia's Galunggung volcano, two jumbo jets filled with passengers lost power when ash stopped their engines. The planes dropped 7,600 m before their pilots were able to restart the engines.

Hot, falling ash can bury roads, clog car engines and knock down electric power lines. Ash can even crush buildings, especially if rain makes it wet and heavy. In the 1991 eruption of Mount Pinatubo in the Philippines, many people died when their roofs collapsed under huge amounts of ash.

When ash covers farmers' fields, it can destroy crops and cause famines. Famines are serious food shortages that cause people to die from starvation. Thousands of people starved after the 1815 eruption of Indonesia's Tambora volcano.

Lightning flashes above the slopes of Galunggung *(top)*. Both lightning and volcanic ash can be big problems for aeroplanes *(bottom)*.

"The rich, green rice paddies had turned into grey-white desert. . . . Refugees trudged nowhere through hot, dusty ash, a half-foot (15 cm) thick or more."

– reporter Susan Kreifels, describing the eruption of Mount Pinatubo in 1991

BARBARA ELEMENTARY SCH

A school was still buried up to its roof in ash, five months after Mount Pinatubo's 1991 eruption.

1883 KRAKATAU

Krakatau erupted in 1883.

The volcano on the Indonesian island of Krakatau had been asleep for centuries. When it erupted in 1883, crowds began gathering outside to watch the natural fireworks show each night. Light from red-hot lava reflected off glowing clouds of dust and gas. Fingers of lightning flashed. But the fireworks soon turned into a horror show.

Beginning at 10.02 am on 26 August and lasting until the next night, Krakatau blew itself apart. The ear-splitting explosions may have been the loudest sounds ever heard by humans. They could be heard 4,830 km (3,000 miles) away, almost the distance from London to New York.

'**Suddenly, it became pitch dark,**' wrote Mrs Beyerinck. She was on the nearby island of Sumatra with her children when blasts of hot gas and ash swept in. '**The last thing I saw was the ash being pushed up through cracks in the floorboards, like a fountain.**' When she ran outside into the hot ash cloud, it burned her badly. '**I noticed . . . that my skin was hanging off everywhere. I wanted to pull bits of skin off, but that was still more painful.**'

The explosions threw huge chunks of Krakatau into the sea, creating waves more than 30 m high. Called tsunamis, these enormous waves raced across the ocean, crashing down on coastal villages. They smashed houses and drowned people and animals.

'**We saw a great black thing, a long way off, coming towards us,**' said a farmer on nearby Java. '**It was very high and very strong, and we soon saw that it was water. Trees and houses were washed away. People began running for their lives.**'

More than 36,000 people died due to Krakatau's eruption. Tens of thousands more were injured.

'All Gone. Plenty Lives Lost'
— a telegraph message sent during Krakatau's eruption

Krakatau affected people all over the world. The dust and gas that it threw into the air reflected sunlight back into space, making the whole planet cooler for several years.

After the devastating 1883 eruption, Krakatau's island was nearly gone. The volcano itself grew quiet, but in 1927, it began erupting again, building a new cone-shaped mountain. People named it Anak Krakatau, meaning 'Child of Krakatau.' Will it one day be as fierce as its parent?

By 2005 Anak Krakatau was almost 300 m high – and still growing.

Volcano Country

MOST OF THE WORLD'S VOLCANOES ARE LOCATED IN A BELT CALLED THE RING OF FIRE. THIS RING MARKS WHERE THE EARTH'S TECTONIC PLATES MEET, GRINDING TOGETHER WITH GREAT FORCE. MANY EARTHQUAKES ALSO OCCUR IN THIS REGION.

The Ring of Fire stretches around the Pacific Ocean, going northwards from Chile to California and Alaska. Then it continues westwards to Japan and the Philippine Islands and finally south to New Zealand. A smaller

VOLCANOES FROM MARS

The Earth is not the only planet with volcanoes. Space missions have found evidence of volcanoes on other planets and moons too. Mars *(left, bottom)* has huge, dormant volcanoes. Some are 27 km (17 miles) high and 560 km (350 miles) wide. Venus also has many volcanoes, and one of Jupiter's moons, Io *(left, top)*, has active, erupting volcanoes. Pictures from unmanned spacecraft show gas and other material billowing up more than 161 km (100 miles) above Io's surface.

amount of volcanic activity also happens outside the Ring of Fire, in places including Iceland, Hawaii and southern Europe.

SLEEPING VOLCANOES

The Earth has about 1,500 active volcanoes on its surface. An active volcano is a volcano that is erupting right now or that has erupted within the last one thousand years or so. Japan has 108 active volcanoes. The United States has 50 – Mount Saint Helens is probably the USA's most famous volcano.

Around the world, many more active volcanoes – up to 10,000 – are hidden from view on the ocean floor. They are called submarine volcanoes.

Hundreds of other volcanoes are dormant. They are sleeping quietly now. But scientists know that they have erupted some time during the last several thousand years and may erupt again. Hawaii's Mauna Kea is a dormant volcano. Other volcanoes are extinct, which means they were once active but have fizzled out and probably will never erupt again. Hawaii's Kohala volcano is believed to be extinct.

It can be hard to tell whether a volcano is extinct or just quietly building up lava underground. Scientists may list a volcano as dormant until they know more about the chances of another eruption.

Scientists use this specialized tool, called a submersible, to study underwater volcanoes.

DISASTER ZONES

Most of the world's volcanoes are located along the Ring of Fire.
This map shows a few of the Earth's hundreds of fire mountains.
The boxed information describes especially important eruptions.

EUROPE

ASIA

AFRICA

AUSTRALIA

VESUVIUS (Italy)
AD 79 (3,300+ deaths)
1631 (3,500+ deaths)

KLYUCHEVSKAYA SOPKA – Russia

FUJI – Japan

UNZEN (Japan)
1792 (14,500+ deaths)

PINATUBO
(Philippines)

ERTA ALE – Ethiopia

TAAL – Philippines

GALUNGGUNG – Indonesia

KILIMANJARO – Tanzania

KRAKATAU (Indonesia)
1883 (36,000 deaths)

NYIRAGONGO
(Democratic Republic of
Congo, formerly Zaire)
2002 (45 deaths)

TAMBORA (Indonesia)
1815 (92,000+ deaths)

LAMINGTON (Papua New Guinea)
1951 (2,942 deaths)

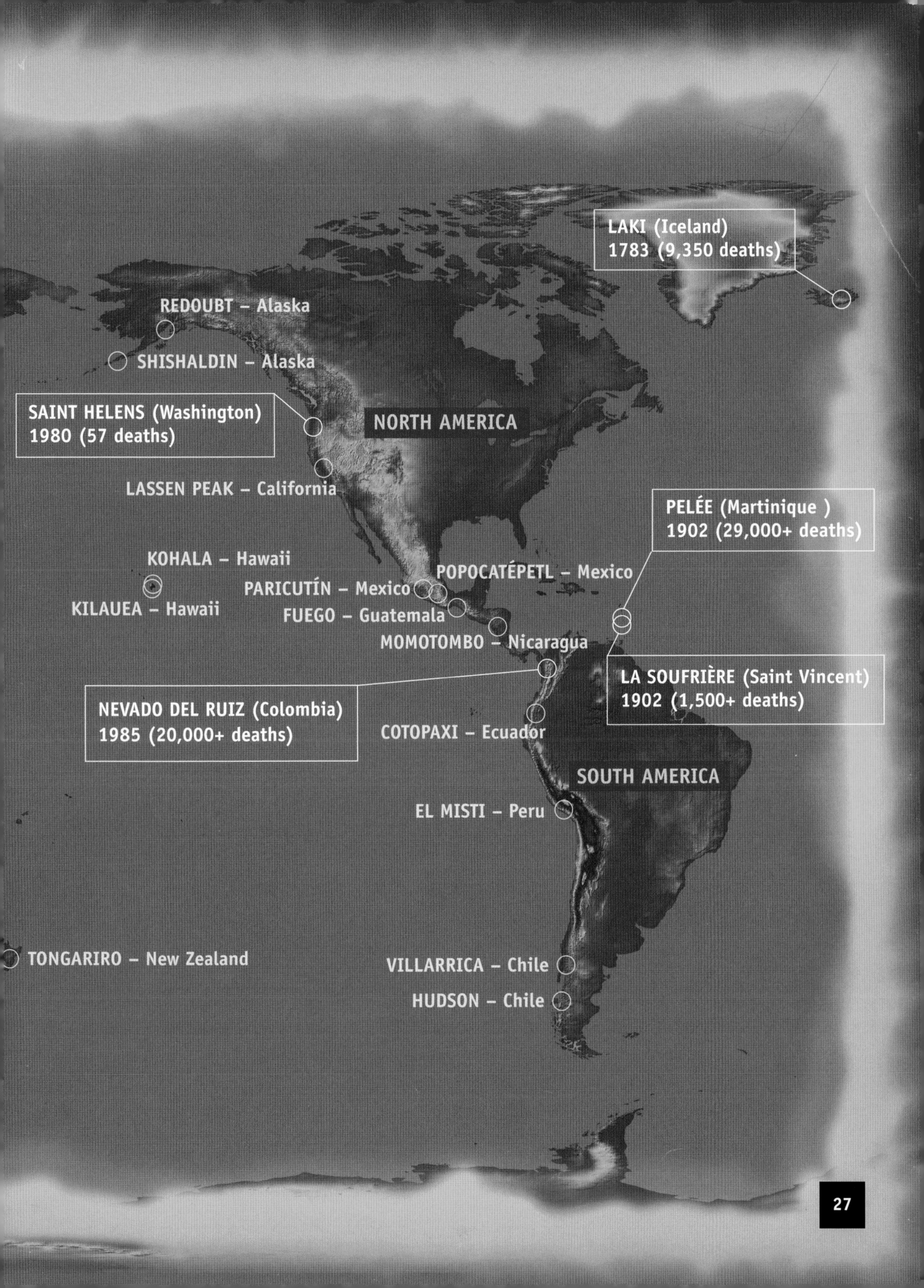

LAKI (Iceland)
1783 (9,350 deaths)

REDOUBT – Alaska

SHISHALDIN – Alaska

SAINT HELENS (Washington)
1980 (57 deaths)

NORTH AMERICA

LASSEN PEAK – California

PELÉE (Martinique)
1902 (29,000+ deaths)

KOHALA – Hawaii

POPOCATÉPETL – Mexico

PARICUTÍN – Mexico

KILAUEA – Hawaii

FUEGO – Guatemala

MOMOTOMBO – Nicaragua

LA SOUFRIÈRE (Saint Vincent)
1902 (1,500+ deaths)

NEVADO DEL RUIZ (Colombia)
1985 (20,000+ deaths)

COTOPAXI – Ecuador

SOUTH AMERICA

EL MISTI – Peru

TONGARIRO – New Zealand

VILLARRICA – Chile

HUDSON – Chile

27

" *I saw that a boiling red river was coming. . . .* "

– *Havivra Da Ifrile*

Mount Pelée

1902 MOUNT PELÉE

The city of Saint Pierre lies at the bottom of the Mount Pelée volcano. Located on the Caribbean island of Martinique, Saint Pierre is usually a beautiful, peaceful tropical spot. But on 8 May 1902, Pelée erupted at 7.50 am.

As the eruption began, thousands of poisonous snakes and insects – including 30-centimetre centipedes – fled from the volcano. They invaded Saint Pierre, biting horses, dogs and people. More than 50 people died from snake and insect bites, but the worst was yet to come.

A huge, glowing-hot cloud of gas, ash and rock rushed down from the volcano, whooshing into Saint Pierre at about 160 kmph. Within just a few minutes, almost everyone in Saint Pierre – more than 29,000 people – had died.

'I felt a terrible wind blowing,' recalled one survivor, a young shoemaker named Léon Compère-Léandre. He was sitting on his doorstep

when the fire mountain erupted. **'The earth began to tremble, and the sky suddenly became dark. I turned to go into the house . . . and felt my arms and legs burning, also my body.'**

Four other people hid inside with Léon, but hot gas burned them all and only Léon survived. When the house caught fire, Léon was able to struggle out. His **'legs bleeding and covered with burns,'** he reached safety in a town 6 km (3.5 miles) away.

Havivra Da Ifrile was outside Saint Pierre that day, doing an errand for her mother. When Mount Pelée erupted, Havivra jumped into her brother's boat and rowed to a small cave nearby.

'Before I got there I looked back,' she remembered. **'The whole side of the mountain . . . seemed to open and boil down on the screaming people. I was burned a good deal by the stones and ashes that came flying about the boat.'**

After Pelée grew quiet, it left a strange and spooky reminder of its destruction. Lava sometimes cools into a pile, or dome. In October 1902, Pelée started forming an unusual dome. Growing as much as 15 m a day, the tower was soon more than 300 m high. People called it the Tower of Pelée. At night, its sides glowed from the red-hot lava inside. It collapsed in March 1903 – but no one forgot the terror of Pelée's disaster.

Scientists examined the destruction caused by Pelée.

This man *(above, left)* survived Pelée's eruption – but he was scarred by burns. Saint Pierre lay in ruins *(left)*.

29

Measuring the Menace

WHEN PEOPLE HEAR THAT A VOLCANO HAS ERUPTED, THEY USUALLY WONDER HOW BIG THE ERUPTION WAS. WERE PEOPLE HURT? DID THE ERUPTION CAUSE A LARGE DISASTER?

That's what Howard Berkes wanted to know when Mount Saint Helens, in the USA erupted in 1980. 'I was in bed, and there was this huge boom,' he recalled. 'I have to tell you, I was 160 miles away . . . but the force of the blast reached us and the windows in my house shook. I fell out of bed.'

Scientists who study volcanoes are called volcanologists. Before, during and after eruptions, volcanologists take many measurements. They use special electronic instruments, or tools. These instruments include seismographs, which measure vibrations and movement in the Earth. Other tools measure how much the surface of the Earth bulges or swells as magma moves under the crust.

TOOLS OF THE TRADE

Volcanologists have an exciting but dangerous job. As they study volcanic activity, they wear heat-resistant suits, gloves and helmets to protect themselves from the fiery heat of lava and volcanic gases. They also use special thermometers to measure the temperature of lava – ordinary thermometers would melt!

A volcanologist collects a lava sample from Hawaii's Mauna Ulu. He wears special clothes to protect his body from the lava's heat.

Volcanologists working at Mount Saint Helens took measurements of a lava dome that began growing after the 1980 eruption.

"Sometimes we felt **dozens** of earthquakes in a single day, which sort of keeps you on edge."

— Christina Heliker, a volcanologist who worked at Mount Saint Helens

Some instruments take samples of gas released by volcanoes. Scientists also collect samples of magma and lava to see what kinds of melted rock and minerals it contains. All of this information tells us more about how volcanoes form and erupt.

Once a volcano does erupt, scientists measure the eruption with a scale called the Volcanic Explosivity Index (VEI). The VEI tells people about the size of an eruption. It also gives scientists a way to compare one eruption to another. The VEI describes small eruptions as non-explosive and gentle. Big eruptions are called colossal, super-colossal and mega-colossal.

However, the VEI does not tell us anything about how much damage eruptions cause to humans. For example, if a volcano erupts where nobody lives, it may cause little damage even if the eruption has a high VEI score.

RANKING A FIRE MOUNTAIN

Scientists work out VEI scores for volcanic eruptions. An eruption's score is based on how explosive the eruption was, as well as the amount of ash that poured out of the volcano. The VEI also takes into account how high ash and gas rise into the atmosphere. When scientists assign VEI scores to past eruptions, they estimate the score based on the amount of damage that was recorded and what eyewitnesses saw. In modern times, they use measurements taken before, during and after an eruption. For example, tools called spectrometers measure how much gas a volcano releases.

Most eruptions have a VEI score between 0 and 8. Each number on the scale also has a ranking, from non-explosive to

BRAINTEASER

Volcanic eruption A had a VEI of 4. Eruption B was an 8 on the VEI scale. How much stronger was B?

You might think that B was twice as strong as A. But it was actually 10,000 times stronger! That's because the VEI is a logarithmic scale. Every increase of one whole number – from 4 to 5, for instance – means an eruption that is 10 times stronger. So eruption B was really $10 \times 10 \times 10 \times 10$ (10,000 times) stronger than A.

Volcanologists take a sample of volcanic gases at Mount Baker in Washington State, USA.

mega-colossal. The VEI calls an eruption of 0 VEI a non-explosive eruption. It does not involve any explosions. It releases less than 1000 cubic m of ash. The ash cloud rises less than about 100 m into the air. Volcanoes with a ranking of 0 VEI may erupt often – maybe even every day. Mount Kilauea in Hawaii is this kind of volcano. It has been erupting ever so gently, almost constantly, since 1983.

Severe eruptions receive a VEI of 3. They release at least 10 million cubic m of ash in a cloud that rises 3 to 15 km high (2 to 9 miles). In Colombia, the Nevado del Ruiz's 1985 eruption scored a 3 on the VEI scale. Eruptions with a VEI of 6 are colossal. They release at least 10 cubic km (2.5 cubic miles) of ash. Krakatau's 1883 eruption was ranked as colossal.

MEGA-COLOSSAL ERUPTIONS

Mega-colossal eruptions, which are 8 on the VEI scale, release thousands of cubic kilometres of lava, ash and other material. The ash cloud rises more than 25 km (15.5 miles) into the atmosphere. But they happen only once in tens of thousands of years. The last mega-colossal eruptions occurred about two million years ago in what became Yellowstone National Park in the USA. These violent eruptions helped create the park's beautiful valleys and mountains.

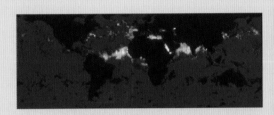

These satellite images show ash from Mount Pinatubo's 1991 eruption spreading around the globe. This eruption ranked as a 6 on the VEI scale.

Deep underneath Yellowstone, an ancient lake of melted rock still exists. It is about 65 km (40 miles) wide. Its heat makes water boil up from the ground in hot springs and geysers (fountains of water that spurt from the ground). Old Faithful, the most famous geyser, pours out a stream of hot water every thirty-five minutes to two hours. These effects of Yellowstone's volcanic activity are largely harmless and often spectacular, but if the underground volcano erupts again, it could cause a great disaster.

Geysers in Yellowstone National Park offer clues to volcanic activity in the area. Yellowstone was the site of a mega-colossal eruption two million years ago.

VEI	DESCRIPTION	HEIGHT OF ASH CLOUD	VOLUME OF MATERIAL EJECTED	FREQUENCY OF ERUPTION	EXAMPLE
0	NON-EXPLOSIVE	<100 M	1,000 M³	DAILY	KILAUEA
1	GENTLE	100–1000 M	10,000s M³	DAILY	STROMBOLI
2	EXPLOSIVE	1–5 KM	1,000,000s M³	WEEKLY	GALERAS, 1993
3	SEVERE	3–15 KM	10,000,000s M³	YEARLY	NEVADO DEL RUIZ, 1985
4	CATACLYSMIC	10–25 KM	100,000,000s M³	10s OF YEARS	GALUNGGUNG, 1982
5	PAROXYSMAL	>25 KM	1 KM³	100s OF YEARS	SAINT HELENS, 1980
6	COLOSSAL	>25 KM	10s KM³	100s OF YEARS	KRAKATAU, 1883
7	SUPER-COLOSSAL	>25 KM	100s KM³	1000s OF YEARS	TAMBORA, 1815
8	MEGA-COLOSSAL	>25 KM	1,000s KM³	10,000s OF YEARS	YELLOWSTONE, 2 MILLION YEARS AGO

* The symbol < means 'less than' and > means 'greater than.'

1980 MOUNT SAINT HELENS

Eruption of
Mount Saint Helens

One beautiful spring morning, Robert and Mary Barrett were fishing near Mount Saint Helens in Washington State, USA. The weather was warm and the sky bright blue.

'Suddenly, an eerie quiet surrounded us,' Robert said. 'No insect noise, no birds chirped, the fish completely stopped biting, my watch stopped, and the sky began to darken. We looked at each other and said in unison, "The mountain"!'

Yes – the fire mountain. Mount Saint Helens had been dormant since 1857. However, in March 1980, it showed signs of awakening. Scientists and curious citizens started keeping watch on the mountain. Hundreds of people were gathered on May 18, hoping to watch the mild eruption that scientists had expected for weeks. Instead, Mount Saint Helens blew its top.

A violent explosion tore 400 m of earth and rock off the mountain's peak. It released a blast of searing-hot gas and ash, knocking down trees as if they were matchsticks. David Johnston, a US

Mudflows from Mount Saint Helens nearly submerged these mailboxes.

Geological Survey scientist, was 10 km (6 miles) from the eruption. **'This is it!'** he said on his radio – just moments before the blast wave's force and burning heat killed him.

Lava streams of 650°C flowed down the volcano's slopes, destroying everything they touched. Lava piled up 40 m deep in places as it cooled. Huge amounts of hot ash poured out of the volcano, forming a cloud that rose 25,000 m into the air within fifteen minutes. Ash blocked out the sun, and the bright day seemed to turn into night. **'Pouring out of the gaping hole in the mountain was this just constant flow of ash and rock and smoke,'** remembered Howard Berkes.

'It began to look like snow falling,' said Ramona Hopkins, who was 400 km (250 miles) away. **'It was pitch black.'** Thousands of people were stranded when ash blocked roads and clogged car and aeroplane engines. Some people escaped by driving cars at 160 kmph, keeping just ahead of the blast. The eruption caused the biggest avalanche ever recorded on Earth. A rush of rocks and dirt buried people, animals and forests up to 25 km (17 miles) away. In all, the Mount Saint Helens' disaster killed 57 people.

A bird killed by the eruption lay on an ash-covered city street *(above, left)*, while regional newspapers carried frightening headlines *(left)*.

37

People Helping People

PEOPLE WHO SURVIVE A DISASTER USUALLY NEED HELP TO RECOVER. RECOVERY MEANS GETTING LIFE BACK TO NORMAL AGAIN. VOLCANIC ERUPTIONS AND OTHER DISASTERS MAY INJURE OR KILL FAMILY MEMBERS, FRIENDS AND PETS. DISASTERS CAN ALSO DESTROY PEOPLES' HOMES. SOMETIMES EVERYTHING THAT THEY OWNED IS GONE.

'I'm not happy because now I have no job, no home, no money and very few clothes,' said Mwendi Kambale. Her family lost their home in the 2002 eruption of Mount Nyiragongo in the Democratic Republic of Congo.

Survivors of volcanic eruptions may need water, food, clothing, warm blankets and a place to live until new homes can be built. Wreckage has to be cleared away before new buildings can be constructed. Workers must fix broken water pipes and restore power and telephone services. Roads and bridges must be repaired. To do all of these things, people have to help one another.

A Goma woman carried a container of lake water for drinking and cleaning after the Nyiragongo eruption.

NEIGHBOURS HELPING NEIGHBOURS

Help is not always available right away. After a disaster, roads may be blocked and airports closed. Emergency rescue personnel and police might be unable to reach the disaster scene quickly.

Children in the African country of Cameroon lined up to receive aid after a lake released toxic volcanic gases into the air in 1986. More than 1,700 people died.

At first, people often have to help themselves and one another, but doing this can be especially difficult right after a disaster. People feel a sense of shock that such a terrible thing has happened.

'People were walking in circles,' recalled Dr Diva Cuartas. Dr Cuartas lived near the town of Guayabal, Colombia. The town was covered with mud after Colombia's Nevado del Ruiz volcano erupted in 1985.

After the Nevado del Ruiz disaster, survivors tried to help their neighbours, but often they could not. As José Luis Restrepo remembered, 'We saw that horrible sea of mud, which was so gigantic. . . there were people buried, calling out, calling for help, and if you tried to go to them, you would sink in the mud.'

Dr Cuartas and five other doctors from the area set up a hospital near Guayabal and started treating injured people. In the first two days after the disaster, people from Bogotá, Colombia's capital, sent all kinds of aid, from rolls of plastic to make tents to blankets, clothing and medicine. A soft drinks company donated 100,000 bottles of water and 30,000 twelve-packs of fizzy drinks.

HOW CAN YOU HELP?

Even if you can't reach disaster victims in person, you can still help. Many people donate money to groups that send relief teams and supplies to disaster struck areas around the world. The International Red Cross is one of the best-known groups. To find out more, visit their website at http://www.redcross.org. The United Nations' ReliefWeb site at http://www.reliefweb.int/ is another good resource, especially for international disasters.

Aid agencies bring water and nourishment to volcano victims, such as this survivor of the Nyiragongo eruption.

Even when eruptions aren't fatal, they can cause big changes and problems for nearby communities. This enormous lava flow blocked a main road in Hawaii.

GETTING LIFE BACK TO NORMAL

When a disaster occurs, members of the fire service and police force are usually the first rescue workers to arrive on the scene. They provide first aid to injured people, put out fires, and work in other ways to keep the damage from getting worse. Relief workers from the Red Cross and Red Crescent Movement may also rush to the scene. They help provide victims with clean water, food and a place to stay.

Poorer countries often need help from outside. Assistance may come from disaster relief teams sent by other countries. Aid also comes from groups that are organized to provide help in emergencies, such as the Red Cross and CARE International. Within hours of a disaster, they can fly in huge amounts of supplies and hundreds of experienced workers. This help can be especially important in poorer countries that don't have the things they need to deal with disasters.

MONEY MATTERS

One of the most important international relief agencies is the Disasters Emergency Committee. This British based organization provides financial aid to disaster struck areas. It gets its funds from UK businesses, the media sector and public donations. This is divided between 13 aid agencies who distribute the money to where it is needed most.

No matter where a disaster occurs, rescue workers first need help finding victims – as quickly as possible. For example, people may be buried alive under buildings that have fallen down in an earth-shaking eruption. If they are not found quickly and given medical help, they will die. Search and rescue teams do this work. They often use specially trained dogs that sniff out people buried under wreckage. It is also important to recover the bodies of people killed in the disaster. Then family members and friends will be better able to grieve.

Aid workers offered water to Isidro Borques, who was trapped in the ruins of his house after it was destroyed by mudflows from Nevado del Ruiz.

Relief workers often assist with search and rescue efforts. They have a very important job, but it's risky work. A volcano may erupt again at any time. Also lava already on the ground is dangerous. 'Some piles are still hot enough to fry an egg on,' said Wendy Driscoll, who worked at Goma. When lava begins to cool, it forms a dark outer crust that looks solid. But, Wendy said, 'like ice, the surface crust can break to reveal the scorching lava hidden below.'

As lorries and aeroplanes bring in supplies to help survivors, rebuilding begins. Repairing homes and towns is one of the most important steps in recovering from a disaster. It helps people return to their old way of life.

People often rebuild right near an active volcano. It is dangerous to rebuild in a place where disasters are waiting to happen. Mount Nyiragongo, for instance, has damaged the town of Goma in the past, and it probably will do so again. Yet aid workers know that it is important to allow local people to make their own decisions about whether to stay or move.

A house damaged by the eruption of Mount Saint Helens

BETTER DISASTER RELIEF

In the past, survivors of volcanic eruptions often received little or no help. When Mount Vesuvius erupted in AD 79, the Roman navy sent only one small ship to Pompeii and Herculaneum. The sailors rescued important people, but they left quickly and they didn't return.

In modern times, hundreds of disaster relief organizations exist. Many work together at the scene of a disaster. They cooperate to give survivors the help that they need. Disaster relief organizations are trying to find new ways to reach disaster victims even sooner and to help them return to a normal life more quickly.

DISASTROUS BILLS

Disaster relief is expensive. The 1980 eruption of Mount Saint Helens destroyed hundreds of homes and killed millions of trees. The damage and cleanup for that disaster cost more than $1.1 billion.

Workers in the Philippines painstakingly cleaned up the piles of ash left by Mount Pinatubo's 1991 eruption.

Nevado del Ruiz

1985 'MUD' VOLCANO

In the South American country of Colombia, the Nevado del Ruiz volcano rises almost 5,300 m high. A thick layer of snow and ice covers it in a sparkling white blanket all year round. But during the night of 13 November 1985, Ruiz erupted.

The mountain poured 20 million cubic m of hot ash and rocks out onto the snow – enough to fill 2.6 million lorries. As the snow melted and mixed with ash, it formed a lahar. This river of hot mud rushed down Nevado del Ruiz's slopes at 50 kmph, picking up dirt and stones as it went. Some parts of the stream were 40 m wide.

At about 10.30 pm, the lahar hit the town of Armero. The thick, heavy mud was filled with sharp rocks and broken tree branches that cut people and tore off their clothing. In a few short minutes, the mud swept away or buried most of the town. About 25,000 people – three-quarters of Armero's residents – were dead.

When Alba Triviedo heard the mud's roar, she ran outside with her children. *'The mud tore down our house,'* Alba said. *'Everything around us was destroyed, but it didn't touch us. It was a miracle we lived. We walked out by ourselves. We didn't eat or drink for two days.'*

Another survivor, José Luis Restrepo, was on a field trip in Armero when the mudflows swept into town. He remembers, *'We didn't hear any kind of alarm, even when the ash was falling and we were in the hotel. . . . We were running and about to reach the corner when a river of water came down the streets. . . . We turned around, screaming, towards the hotel, because the waters were already dragging beds along, overturning cars, sweeping people away. . . . Suddenly, I heard bangs, and looking towards the rear of the hotel I saw . . . [a wall] of*

The town of Armero was devastated by mudflows.

mud approaching the hotel, and sure enough, it crashed against the rear of the hotel and started crushing walls.'

Thirteen-year-old Omaira Sánchez was among those who did not escape. She was trapped in a hole filled with rocks, mud and water up to her neck. Workers tried to rescue her for more than two days, as millions of people watched on television. Tragically, before the workers could free her, Omaira died from injuries caused by the rocks hitting her body.

Aid workers tried to help Omaira Sánchez.

The Future

FINDING ACCURATE WAYS TO PREDICT ERUPTIONS FURTHER IN ADVANCE IS AN IMPORTANT GOAL OF VOLCANOLOGY (THE STUDY OF VOLCANOES). VOLCANOLOGISTS WANT TO KNOW WHEN AND WHERE THE NEXT ERUPTION WILL HAPPEN AND HOW BIG IT WILL BE. THAT INFORMATION COULD SAVE MANY LIVES.

Scientists can sometimes issue life-saving warnings of volcanic eruptions. By studying past eruptions, they have learned that volcanoes often behave in certain ways before an eruption. Many small earthquakes may occur, for instance, as melted rock rises from deep below the ground. As this magma collects underground and the pressure rises, a volcano's sides may swell. Volcanoes may also warn of an eruption by releasing more ash and gas than usual or different kinds of gas.

NEW TECHNOLOGY

Special scientific tools placed near a volcano can record and measure changes in the volcano's activity. Other tools, located on satellites in orbit high above the Earth, also keep watch on volcanoes. Special radar devices can spot volcanoes hidden under the ground or ocean.

Scientists are working on new ways of using warning signs and measurements to predict eruptions. One goal is to invent new computer programs.

Satellites gather information on volcanic activity from kilometres above the Earth's surface.

Early volcanologists often used simple tools. In 1917 this scientist listens to the sounds made by Italy's Solfatara volcano. Modern volcanologists use sophisticated seismographs to track even the tiniest volcanic rumblings.

These programs will be able to forecast eruptions, in the same way modern weather computers forecast storms. These programs are called computer models. They use measurements of gas, ash and earthquakes to show how a volcano will probably behave.

In the future, volcano models may become as good as the weather models used to predict hurricanes. They would enable officials to issue warnings like this: 'Attention! This is a volcano eruption warning. An eruption is about to happen. Everyone should leave the area as soon as possible.' This kind of warning is not usually possible. In the future, we may be able to make eruption forecasts that are accurate enough to warn people living nearby to evacuate (leave).

Research also may lead to better ways of collecting warning signs from space. Satellites orbiting the Earth might one day carry special sensors that watch all of the Earth's active volcanoes. The satellites would send this information to computers that could then predict eruptions and issue alerts. Other research might not even study volcanoes themselves, but is still very important. Some researchers look for ways to build stronger houses, schools and other buildings that can resist damage from the lava, ash and mud of an eruption.

Two volcanologists arrive at their helicopter after gathering gas, soil and water samples at Mount Pinatubo.

Workers built a dike
near Indonesia's Merapi
volcano to protect against
lava and mudflows in
future eruptions.

PREDICTIONS SAVE LIVES

Volcanology has helped scientists predict eruptions and save lives. Volcanologists predicted the 1980 eruption of Mount Saint Helens three weeks in advance. Radio and television stations broadcast these warnings. People near the mountain had time to evacuate and save their lives. In 1991 scientists said that Mount Pinatubo in the Philippines was about to erupt. About 75,000 people were moved to safe areas. When it erupted, more than 700 people still died, but the prediction saved thousands of others.

Many people have died in the past because warnings were not given or because people did not pay attention. Colombia's Nevado del Ruiz volcano showed signs of an eruption in 1985. Officials, however, were afraid it might be a false alarm. They did not evacuate the town of Armero. When the volcano erupted, thousands of people died in a river of hot mud. Studies of the Nevado del Ruiz eruption also showed that even small eruptions can result in disastrous mudflows from snowcapped volcanoes.

Scientists learn many lessons from previous eruptions. These lessons can keep people safe in the future. By studying past disasters, scientists and governments can see mistakes to avoid in the future. For instance, they can make better plans for evacuating people.

VOLCANO OBSERVATORIES

Observatories are not just for astronomers who study stars and planets. Volcano observatories help scientists predict future eruptions. These buildings are located near active volcanoes. By gathering information over long periods of time, scientists at volcano observatories learn to spot the warning signs of a serious eruption.

A volcanologist with the Alaska Volcano Observatory sets up a scientific station to monitor the Akutan volcano.

A ferry headed towards Japan's Sakurajima volcano, ready to evacuate nearby residents in case of a large eruption.

PLANNING FOR DISASTERS

Volcano eruption warnings are one way of reducing risks to people and property. Another way is encouraging people not to build houses and other buildings too close to active volcanoes. Governments can also require structures in volcanic areas to be built especially strong. Homes, for instance, can have roofs that will not collapse if volcanic ash collects on them.

One of the very best ways to stay safe is having a disaster plan. This written plan explains how a community will respond to a volcanic eruption. It spells out how people will be told about the disaster threat, how they will leave the area, where they will go and who will help them. Without a good plan, even the best forecasts can be useless.

Volcanoes are powerful and, like any disaster, volcanic eruptions can be very frightening. However, being prepared, helping one another and understanding more about how fire mountains affect people can make everyone safer.

These Japanese girls have learned to live in the shadow of an active volcano. They wear hard hats to protect them from the debris that falls frequently.

BE PREPARED

If you live in a volcano danger zone, you and your family can do several things to stay safe.

- Learn about your community's system for warning people about an eruption and about its disaster plan.

- Know the emergency evacuation route. Have a backup route in mind.

- Keep an emergency kit at home and in each vehicle. Include a torch and spare batteries, a battery-powered radio, some water and food and a first-aid kit.

- Remember to pack an extra emergency kit with food and water for pets.

- Prepare for volcanic dust. Each family member should have a disposable breathing mask and a pair of goggles.

- Follow instructions from local emergency officials.

Timeline

AD 79 Mount Vesuvius *(right)* in Italy erupts, burying Pompeii and Herculaneum. The disaster kills more than 3,000 people.

1631 An eruption of Mount Vesuvius kills 4,000 people and demolishes six villages.

1669 Mount Etna, on the Italian island of Sicily, erupts, killing an estimated 20,000.

1783 The Laki volcano in Iceland creates such a dark haze that crops fail and 9,350 people die from starvation.

1792 The eruption of the Mount Unzen volcano on Japan's Kyushu Island becomes the nation's greatest volcano disaster, with most deaths caused by the resulting tsunami.

1815 Mount Tambora in Sumbawa, Indonesia, kills 92,000 people with a combination of the eruption and the resulting starvation and deaths from drinking contaminated water.

1883 The explosion from the Krakatau, Indonesia, eruption is heard as far away as Australia and causes a huge tsunami that kills 36,000 people.

1902 On 7 May, La Soufrière volcano erupts on the Caribbean island of Saint Vincent. The eruption devastates one-third of the island.

On 8 May, molten rock from the eruption of Mount Pelée in Martinique devastates the city of Saint Pierre, killing more than 29,000 people in the city and beyond.

1911 Mount Taal erupts in the Philippines. Ash clouds kill 1,335 people.

1912 Alaska's Novarupta volcano erupts in the largest eruption in the twentieth century, spreading volcanic material thirty times the volume of Mount Saint Helens's 1980 eruption.

1943 Mount Paricutín *(left)* erupts in Mexico. This volcano arose from a flat cornfield and was more than 350m high within a year. By 1952 it appeared to be dormant.

1977 The lava lake at Mount Nyiragongo in the Democratic Republic of Congo develops a leak, burning villages and killing 70 people.

1980 Mount Saint Helens *(left)* erupts in Washington State, USA, killing 57 people and thousands of animals.

1982 The Indonesian Galunggung volcano erupts, spewing volcanic ash that clogs four engines on a British Airways flight to Singapore. The plane falls for eight minutes before the engines are restarted.

1985 Colombia's Nevado del Ruiz volcano erupts and creates mudflows that bury most of the town of Armero, killing almost 25,000 people.

1986 Clouds of carbon dioxide escape from Lake Nyos, located in a volcanic crater in Cameroon, Africa. The gas suffocates 1,700 people and many farm animals.

1989 Volcanic ash from Alaska's Redoubt Volcano causes problems for local air traffic.

1991 Mount Pinatubo *(right)* in the Philippines buries around 750 sq km (300 sq miles) of land under volcanic ash. However, due to coordinated efforts from the US military and local organizations, thousands of people were saved.

1997 The Soufrière Hills volcano on the Caribbean island of Montserrat devastates the island and forces two-thirds of the population to move away.

2002 Lava flows from Mount Nyiragongo volcano leave 500,000 people homeless.

2004–2005 Minor eruptions take place at Mount Saint Helens *(left)*. Volcanologists continue to monitor the volcano's activity.

Glossary

active volcano: a volcano that is erupting right now or that has erupted within the last one thousand years or so

ash: very tiny pieces of rock that rise into the air during a volcanic eruption

dormant volcano: a volcano that is not active but which scientists know has erupted some time during the last several thousand years

eruption: the bursting forth of melted rock, hot gases, ash and chunks of soil and stone from a volcano

evacuate: to leave a dangerous area and go somewhere safe

extinct volcano: a volcano that was once active but has fizzled out and probably will never erupt again

lahar: a pyroclastic flow that contains water. Lahars are also called mudflows.

lava: melted rock that has flowed out of a volcano. Melted rock that has cooled and hardened back into solid rock is also called lava.

magma: melted rock that is still underground and has not flowed out of a volcano

magma chamber: an underground space where magma builds up before erupting from a volcano

observatory: a building, usually located near an active volcano, where scientists watch and study the volcano

pyroclastic flow: a very hot cloud of ash, rock and gas that rushes outwards from a volcano. Pyroclastic flows move like liquid and can travel very quickly.

Ring of Fire: the region where the Earth's tectonic plates meet. Most of the globe's volcanoes are located in this area, which stretches around the Pacific Ocean from North and South America to Asia.

tectonic plates: huge chunks of rock that carry the Earth's continents and oceans. Volcanoes often occur at the boundaries of these plates.

tephra: material that a volcanic eruption hurls into the air. Tephra can contain tiny specks of ash, as well as large rocks.

vent: a hole or crack in the ground

Volcanic Explosivity Index (VEI): a scale that measures the strength of volcanic eruptions

volcanologist: a scientist who studies volcanoes

Places to Visit

The Natural History Museum, London, UK

http://www.bishopmuseum.org

The Natural History Museum in London has an exhibition on volcanoes and earthquakes and a giant model of the Earth showing its core and the magma that rises from it to form volcanoes.

The Science Museum, London, UK

www.sciencemuseum.org.uk

The Science Museum in London has a video exhibition called the 'Forces of Nature 2D'. This short film showcases the awesome spectacle of earthquakes, volcanoes, tsunamis and severe storms

The Auckland Museum, Auckland New Zealand

The Volcanoes exhibition at the Auckland Museum in New Zealand is about both volcanoes in general and the volcanoes of New Zealand in particular. It looks at the history of Auckland's volcanoes, when they have exploded before and also speculates when they may erupt again.

Source Notes

4   Wendy Driscoll, 'Way to Go? Report on Day Four of a Disaster,' *CARE International*, n.d., http://www.careinternational.org.uk/cares _work/where/rwanda/stories/day4report.htm (17 May 2005).

4   Sally Sara, 'A Quagmire of Debris in Goma,' *The World Today*, 25 January 2002, http://www.abc.net.au/worldtoday/stories/s588062 .htm (17 May 2005).

5   Ibid.

5   Driscoll, 'Way to Go?' *CARE International*.

9   Susan Kreifels, 'Escape from Pinatubo,' *Honolulu Star-Bulletin Online Edition*, 24 June 2001, http://starbulletin.com/2001/06/24/ editorial/special.html (5 October 2005).

12 'Mount Vesuvius,' *Exploring the Environment*, n.d., http://www.cotf.edu/ete/modules/ volcanoes/vmtvesuvius.html (17 May 2005).

12–13 'Pliny the Younger: Eruption of Mt. Vesuvius, A.D. 79,' *IDST, Virginia Tech*, n.d., http://www.idst.vt.edu/thbecker/ 1124/pliny.html (17 May 2005).

13 'Mount Vesuvius,' *Exploring the Environment*.

13 'Pliny the Younger,' *Virginia Tech*.

18 Doctor Robert Tilling, Hawaiian Volcano Observatory scientist, personal interview with author Michael Woods, December 1995.

18 Tomas Guillen, 'A Volcano's Toll: Disaster in Colombia,' *Tomas Guillen, M.A.*, n.d., http://fac-staff.seattleu.edu/tomasg/reporter/ volcano.html (17 May 2005).

21 Kreifels, 'Escape from Pinatubo,' *Honolulu Star-Bulletin*.

22 'Krakatau, Indonesia (1883),' *San Diego State University Department of Geological Sciences*, n.d., http://www.geology.sdsu.edu/how_volcanoes _work/Krakatau.html (17 May 2005).

22   Ibid.

22   Simon Winchester, *Krakatau: The Day the World Exploded. 27 August 1883* (New York: HarperCollins, 2003), 258.

28   'Mt. Pelée Eruption (1902),' *San Diego State University Department of Geological Sciences,* n.d., http://www.geology.sdsu.edu/how_volcanoes_work/Pelee.html (17 May 2005).

28   Ibid.

29   Ibid.

30   'The Reports,' *The Mt. St. Helens Web Site,* n.d., http://www.openix.com/~johnfh3/newpage1.htm (17 May 2005).

31   Tari Mattox, 'Interview with Christina Heliker,' *Volcano World,* 21 May 1999, http://volcano.und.nodak.edu/vwdocs/interview/Christina.html (17 May 2005)

36   Robert Barrett, 'Bass Tournament Stopped by Volcano,' *kitsapsun.com,* n.d., http://www.thesunlink.com/packages/helens/letter3.html (18 May 2005).

37   Stefan Lovgren, 'Mount St. Helens Volcanic Eruptions: 1980 vs. Now,' *National Geographic News,* 7 October 2004, http://news.nationalgeographic.com/news/2004/10/1007_041007_mtsthelens_recap.html (17 May 2005).

37   'The Reports,' *The Mt. St. Helens Web Site.*

37   Ramona Hopkins, 'Lives Put on Hold,' *kitsapsun.com,* n.d., http://www.thesunlink.com/packages/helens/letter1.html, (18 May 2005).

38   'Aid Arrives for Volcano Victims,' *BBC News: Africa,* 22 January 2002, http://news.bbc.co.uk/1/hi/world/africa/1773913.stm (17 May 2005).

40   Guillen, 'A Volcano's Toll,' *Tomas Guillen, M.A.*

40   Alwyn Scarth, *Vulcan's Fury: Man Against the Volcano* (New Haven, CT: Yale University Press, 1999), 241.

44   Driscoll, 'Way to Go?' *CARE International.*

46–47   Guillen, 'A Volcano's Toll,' *Tomas Guillen, M.A.*

47   Scarth, *Vulcan's Fury,* 239–240.

Selected Bibliography

ABS-CBN. 'Pinatubo Volcano: The Sleeping Giant Awakens.' N.d. http://parallel.park.org/Philippines/pinatubo (17 May 2005).

American National Red Cross. 'Disaster Services.' American Red Cross. N.d. http://www.redcross.org/services/disaster (17 May 2005).

De Boer, Jelle Zeilinga, and Donald Theodore Sanders. *Volcanoes in Human History: The Far Reaching Effects of Major Eruptions.* Princeton, NJ: Princeton University Press, 2002.

Ewert, John W., C. Dan Miller, James W. Hendley II, and Peter H. Stauffer. 'Mobile Response Team Saves Lives in Volcano Crises.' *USGS.* N.d. http://pubs.usgs.gov/fs/1997/fs064-97/ (17 May 2005).

Hancock, Paul L., and Brian J. Skinner. *The Oxford Companion to the Earth.* New York: Oxford University Press, 2000.

Johnson, Carl. *Fire on the Mountain.* San Francisco: Chronicle Books, 1994.

McGuire, Bill. *Raging Planet: Earthquakes, Volcanoes, and the Tectonic Threat to Life on Earth.* Hauppauge, NY: Barron's Educational Series, 2002.

Ritchie, David, and Alexander E. Gates. *Encyclopedia of Earthquakes and Volcanoes.* New York: Facts on File, 2001.

Seach, John. *Volcano Eruption News.* N.d. http://www .volcanolive.com/volcanolive.html (17 May 2005).

Simkin, Tom, and Lee Siebert. *Volcanoes of the World.* Tucson, AZ: Geoscience Press, 1994.

Smithsonian Institution. *Global Volcanism Program.* N.d. http://www.volcano.si.edu (17 May 2005).

Vogel, Carole G. *Nature's Fury: Eyewitness Reports of Natural Disasters.* New York: Scholastic, 2000.

'Volcanoes.' *New Book of Popular Science.* Danbury, CT: Grolier, 2000.

Ward, Kaari, ed. *Great Disasters: Dramatic True Stories of Nature's Awesome Powers.* Pleasantville, NY: Reader's Digest Association, 1989.

Further Resources

BOOKS

Baldwin, Carol. *Earth Erupts: Volcanoes* (Turbulent Planet) Raintree Publishers, 2004.

Colson, Mary. *Shaky Ground: Earthquakes* (Freestyle Express: Turbulent Planet) Raintree, 2005.

Dixon, Dougal. *Volcano Evacuation* (Expedition Earth) Ticktock Media Ltd, 2004.

Ganeri, Anita. *Volcano!* (Nature's Fury) Franklin Watts Ltd, 2006.

Lawrence, Caroline. *The Secrets of Vesuvius* (Roman Mysteries) Puffin Books, 2004.

Rae, Alison. *Earthquakes and Volcanoes* (Looking at Landscapes) Evans Brothers Ltd, 2005.

Spilsbury, Louise and Richard Spilsbury. *Violent Volcanoes* (Awesome Forces of Nature) Heinemann Library, 2004.

Steele, Chris. *Volcanoes* (Nature on the Rampage) Raintree, 2004.

Steele, Philip. *Volcanoes* (Snapping-Turtle Guides) Ticktock Media Ltd, 2004.

Turnbull, Stephanie. *Volcanoes* (Usborne Beginners) Usborne Publishing Ltd, 2007.

Van Rose, Susanna. *Volcanoes and Earthquakes* (DK Eyewitness Books) DK Publishing, 2004.

Violent Planet (Phenomena) Tictock Media Ltd, 2006.

Waldron, Melanie. *Volcanoes* (Mapping Earthforms) Heinemann Library, 2008.

Waters, Fiona. *Volcanoes* (Our Violent Earth) Hodder Wayland, 2005.

WEBSITES & FILMS

BBC, Science and Nature: Hot Topics

http://www.bbc.co.uk/science/hottopics/naturald-isasters/volcanoes.shtml.

This website has loads of information about volcanoes as well as other disasters such as earthquakes, tornadoes and tsunamis.

CBBC Newsround: Volcanoes

http://news.bbc.co.uk/cbbcnews/hi/find_out/guides/tech/volcanoes/newsid_1768000/1768595.stm

Check out this site for fast facts about volcanoes.

Old Faithful Geyser Webcam

http://www.nps.gov/yell/oldfaithfulcam.htm

Check this site for the next predicted eruption of Yellowstone National Park's most famous geyser and watch online!

Volcanoes

http://www.learner.org/exhibits/volcanoes/

From an educational network of websites, this page looks at the question of whether or not we will ever be able to predict volcanic eruptions accurately.

Volcano Expedition

http://www.sio.ucsd.edu/volcano

Follow along on a January 2001 expedition to Costa Rica, a country along the Ring of Fire.

Volcano World

http://volcano.und.nodak.edu/vw.html

Find history, interviews with real volcanologists, and answers to frequently asked questions at this website

Dantes Peak. Universal Pictures, 1997. Re-released in 2007. This disaster film stars Pearce Brosnan as a volcanologist trying to save the town Dantes Peak from an impending volcanic explosion.

Krakatau, East of Java. Metro-Goldwyn-Mayer, 1969. Re-released, 2005. This old disaster film is exciting – even though it has a disastrous title. Krakatau actually is located west of the island of Java!

Supervolcano. Discovery Channel, 2005. This TV film takes a look at what might happen if the volcano that created Yellowstone erupts again.

Index

Photo Acknowledgements

The photos in this book are used with the permission of: PhotoDisc/Getty Images, pp 1, 3, 14, 15, 20 (bottom), 55, 57 (middle); © Reuters/CORBIS, pp 4, 38, 40, 43; © Krafft/Photo Researchers, Inc., p 5; © Royalty-Free/CORBIS, p 6; © age fotostock/SuperStock, p 7; © Michael S. Yamashita/CORBIS, p 8; © Alberto Garcia/CORBIS, p 9; NOAA, pp 10, 34, 56 (bottom), 57 (top); © Roger Ressmeyer/CORBIS, pp 11, 13 (bottom), 25, 45, 50, 51, 53, 54; Library of Congress, pp 12 (LC-DIG-ppmsc-06584), 28 (LC-USZ62-76173), 29 (left-LC-USZ62-75513), (right-LC-USZ62-75912), 49 (LC-USZ62-76679), 56 top (LC-DIG-ppmsc-06584); © Araldo de Luca/CORBIS, p 13 (top); © SuperStock, Inc./SuperStock, p 17; © Stan Celestian/Glendale Community College, p 18; © Jacques Langevin/CORBIS SYGMA, pp 19, 47 (both); © CORBIS, pp 20 (top), 22, 48; © Les Stone/Sygma/CORBIS, p 21; © Sergio Dorantes/CORBIS, p 23; NASA, p 24 (both); © Rykoff Collection/CORBIS, p 29 (top); US Geological Survey Photo Library, pp 30, 31, 33, 36, 37 (top), 44, 57 (bottom); © T Craddock/zefa/CORBIS, p 35; © Douglas Kirkland/CORBIS, p 37 (middle); © Gary Braasch/CORBIS, p 37 (bottom); © Peter Turnley/CORBIS, p 39; © Bettmann/CORBIS, p 41; © Todd Strand/Independent Picture Service, p 42; © Victor Englebert, p 46; US Geological Survey Photo Library/Game McGimsey, p 52. Diagram by © Bill Hauser/Independent Picture Service, p 15.

Front and Back cover: PhotoDisc/Getty Images.

This book was first published in the United States of America in 2007.

Text copyright © 2007 by Michael Woods and Mary B Woods

About the Authors

Michael Woods is a science and medical journalist in Washington, D. C., who has won many national writing awards. He works in the Washington Bureau of the *Pittsburgh Post-Gazette* and the *Toledo Blade*. Mary B Woods has been a librarian in the Fairfax County Public School System in Virginia and the Benjamin Franklin International School in Barcelona, Spain. Michael's and Mary's other books include the eight-volume Ancient Technology series. Mary and Michael have four children. When not writing, reading, or enjoying their grandchildren, they travel to gather material for future books.